CORNERSTONES OF FREEDOM™

The CIVIL RIGHTS MOVEMENT

BY JENNIFER ZEIGER

CHILDREN'S PRESS®
An Imprint of Scholastic Inc.
New York Toronto London Auckland Sydney
Mexico City New Delhi Hong Kong
Danbury, Connecticut

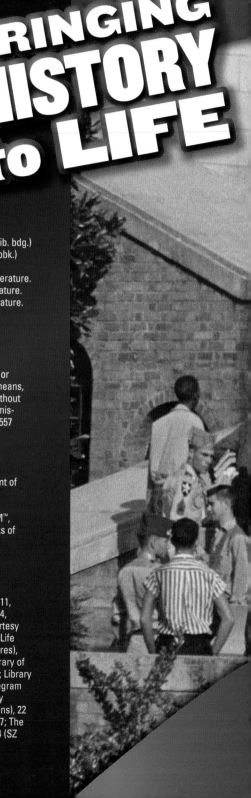

BRINGING HISTORY to LIFE

Content Consultant
Cornelius L. Bynum
Assistant Professor of History
Purdue University
West Lafayette, Indiana

Library of Congress Cataloging-in-Publication Data

Zeiger, Jennifer.
  The civil rights movement/by Jennifer Zeiger.
    p. cm.—(Cornerstones of freedom)
  Includes bibliographical references and index.
  ISBN-13: 978-0-531-25029-7 (lib. bdg.)   ISBN-10: 0-531-25029-6 (lib. bdg.)
  ISBN-13: 978-0-531-26554-3 (pbk.)   ISBN-10: 0-531-26554-4 (pbk.)
  1. African Americans—Civil rights—History—Juvenile literature.
  2. African American civil rights workers—Biography—Juvenile literature.
  3. African American political activists—Biography—Juvenile literature.
  4. Civil rights movements—United States—History—Juvenile literature.
  5. United States—Race relations—Juvenile literature.
  I. Title. II. Series.
  E185.61.Z45 2011
  323.1196'073—dc22   2011016233

Photographs © 2012: AP Images: 49 (Horst Faas), 17, 56 top (Gene
Herrick), 24 (Bill Hudson), 16 (Ed Reinke), 27, 58 (STR), 4 bottom, 8, 11,
25, 26, 42, 51, 59 bottom; Corbis Images/Bettmann: 2, 3, 15, 23, 36, 44,
47, 59 top; Everett Collection, Inc./CSU Archives: 5 bottom, 30; Courtesy
of the FBI: 37; Getty Images: cover (AFP), 18 (Don Cravens/Time & Life
Pictures), 48 (Hulton Archive), 28 (Lee Lockwood/Time & Life Pictures),
46 (MPI), 32 (Rolls Press/Popperfoto), 20 (Marion Post Wolcott/Library of
Congress); Jennifer Zeiger: 64; Landov, LLC/Jim Bourg/Reuters: 55; Library
of Congress: 38 (Warren K. Leffler), 5 top, 45 (New York World-Telegram
& Sun Collection), 12, 56 bottom; NEWSCOM/SHNS photo courtesy
Birmingham Post Herald: 34; Photo Researchers, NY: 10 (Mary Evans), 22
(Bruce Roberts); Superstock, Inc./Everett Collection: back cover, 57; The
Image Works: 35, 39 (Matt Herron/Take Stock), 6 (Roger-Viollet), 14 (SZ
Photo), 40 (Topham), 4 top, 13 (ullstein bild).

Scholastic Inc., 557 Broadway, New York, NY 10012.

Did you know that studying history can be fun?

BRING HISTORY TO LIFE by becoming a history investigator. Examine the evidence (primary and secondary source materials); cross-examine the people and witnesses. Take a look at what was happening at the time—but be careful! What happened years ago might suddenly become incredibly interesting and change the way you think!

Contents

Slavery and Segregation

The Ku Klux Klan dressed in white hooded gowns for its rallies. The KKK had millions of members at the height of its power.

The end of the American Civil War spelled the end of slavery in the United States. When the 13th Amendment to the U.S. Constitution was adopted in December 1865,

THE 13TH AMENDMENT FREED

slavery was officially outlawed. The 14th Amendment was adopted three years later. It granted citizenship to recently freed slaves and was designed to further protect their rights. In 1870, the 15th Amendment gave all African American men the right to vote.

Slavery had ended, but racism had not. White **supremacists,** who believed African Americans were inferior, joined groups such as the Ku Klux Klan (KKK). They organized across the South to limit the effectiveness of the new laws. African Americans, especially those living in the South, were often threatened, beaten, or killed. Laws limited what African Americans could do and where they could go. The laws were intended to **segregate** white and black Americans. Many African Americans were also kept from voting. They were given reading tests many could not pass, or were required to pay a tax they could not afford, before registering to vote. The whites giving the tests would often fail African Americans even though they were able to read. Separated from white society and unable to vote, African Americans had limited power to improve their status. But as the years passed, black and white leaders began to find ways to overcome these limitations.

FIRST STEPS

Before the civil rights movement, African American people were prevented from using many of the facilities used by white people.

IN 1896, THE U.S. SUPREME
Court ruled in the case of *Plessy v. Ferguson*
that segregation was legal. Businesses and
governments could set up separate facilities for
African Americans on the condition that they were
of equal quality to the facilities for white people.
The "separate but equal" rule could be applied
anywhere. Schools, restaurants, department
stores, train stations and train cars, buses, and
even drinking fountains were designated either for
"Whites" or for "Colored," a term commonly used
for African Americans at the time. In reality, the
facilities were rarely of equal quality.

The NAACP, pictured here in 1933, worked to improve education opportunities for African Americans.

The Issue of Education

In many places across the country, white and African American children attended separate schools. The schools were supposed to be equal, but usually they were not. Education in African American schools was often extremely poor. With little money from the government, these schools could not afford books or enough good teachers. The school buildings were often in disrepair because the local governments did not provide enough money for their proper maintenance.

The National Association for the Advancement of Colored People (NAACP) fought court battles to improve the state of education. The NAACP is an organization that was created to support **civil rights**. In 1954, the NAACP won a major battle. In *Brown v. the Board of Education of Topeka, Kansas*, the Supreme Court ruled against segregation in education, overturning *Plessy v. Ferguson*. Thurgood Marshall of the NAACP argued the case. He would later become a U.S. Supreme Court justice. The Supreme Court concluded that "the doctrine of 'separate but equal' has no place" in education.

With segregation in schools now officially illegal, schools had to **integrate** students. Although the Supreme Court demanded integration, the judges did not say when integration had to take place. They merely recommended that it take place "with all deliberate

Thurgood Marshall (center) and two NAACP colleagues after the Supreme Court ruled segregation to be unconstitutional on May 17, 1954.

SPOTLIGHT ON

The NAACP

The National Association for the Advancement of Colored People was created in 1909 in response to the violent practices of terrorist groups such as the Ku Klux Klan. Several civil rights leaders, including author and **activist** W. E. B. DuBois (above), organized the NAACP. DuBois and his associates worked on changing the law to no longer allow discrimination. The NAACP still works today to support African Americans and other minorities seeking better treatment under the law.

speed." No one knew exactly what that meant, but the ruling would soon be tested.

The Little Rock Nine

Some schools quietly integrated, but others refused. States in the South said it could take several years before the time was right. School boards said the public might react violently to a sudden change. Daisy Lee Gatson Bates, the president of the NAACP in Arkansas, took on the challenge. After three years of pushing Arkansas schools to integrate, Bates convinced Central High School in Little Rock to open its doors to black students.

Bates handpicked nine African American students to be the first to attend the school. They were smart, responsible, and tough enough to stand up to the pressure of what lay ahead. The group, which became known as the Little Rock Nine, entered Central High in 1957. They were the first students to integrate a school in the South.

White students and the Arkansas National Guard at first prevented the nine black students from entering Central High School.

On the first day of classes, September 4, the Arkansas National Guard surrounded the school on the orders of Arkansas governor Orval Faubus. The nine had arranged to meet and walk in together, but one of the students did not receive the message. As a result, she found herself in the middle of an angry white mob and was kept out of the school by the armed guardsmen. She was rushed to safety. Nineteen days later, the students tried again to enter, this time together. The mob and the guard again surrounded the school. The nine were again rushed out.

President Eisenhower Steps In

By this time, President Dwight D. Eisenhower had seen enough. For the first time since the Civil War, a president put the country's military to work against its own people. Taking control of the National Guard away from Governor Faubus, Eisenhower had members of the U.S. Army's 101st Airborne Division join their ranks. Under orders from the president, the National Guard and army troops held back the crowds.

U.S. Army troops forced away white crowds who were preventing the black students from entering the school.

The Little Rock Nine were eventually able to attend Central High School.

The army remained at the school to protect the Little Rock Nine until November. For the rest of the year, the students faced constant threats. The school kept all nine of them separated, in different classes all day. At the end of the school year, the state closed all Little Rock public schools. The schools remained closed for an entire year. In 1959, this last attempt by the Arkansas government to halt integration was overcome. The Supreme Court declared that closing the schools was against the law. In the fall, the schools opened again, this time to whites and African Americans alike.

TODAY'S PERSPECTIVE

Many people are still fighting for school integration. In some cities, African Americans and other minorities are isolated in certain neighborhoods. Poor neighborhoods may have few resources to improve schools. Some cities are trying to solve this problem by redrawing the boundary lines that determine which schools students in different neighborhoods attend. By doing this, they hope to achieve more **diversity**, or a better mix of students from different backgrounds, at each school.

In 2007, the Supreme Court blocked two cities' plans for this kind of integration. The judges argued that they were not against integration, but that the plans would not work as well as hoped. Debate about the court's decision continues to this day.

A Seat on the Bus

On December 1, 1955, an African American named Rosa Parks took a seat on a bus in Montgomery, Alabama. Buses in Montgomery, as elsewhere in the South, were segregated. Seats in the front were reserved for white passengers. African Americans were to sit in the back. If the bus was crowded, African American passengers were required to give up their seats to whites. The bus Parks was on was crowded.

When the bus driver asked her to move so a white passenger could sit, Parks politely refused. It was her right, she claimed, as a paying passenger. The police were called, and Parks was arrested.

Rosa Parks became a symbol of the civil rights movement when she refused to give up her bus seat.

The NAACP and other organizations promptly came to support Parks. NAACP lawyers fought her case. Meanwhile, a brief **boycott** of the bus service was planned. Buses and other forms of public transportation would not be used for one day. This would demonstrate the importance of the African American community to the public transportation system. On December 5, approximately 40,000 African Americans bus riders living in Montgomery boycotted the system. Buses drove around all day, nearly or completely empty.

During the Montgomery bus boycott, people walked to work. The boycott showed that peaceful protest could be effective.

The Boycott Expands

Seeing the success of the boycott encouraged the African American community to take further action. A much longer bus boycott was planned. To organize it, the Montgomery Improvement Association (MIA) was created. The Reverend Dr. Martin Luther King Jr. was placed in charge. The 26-year-old King was a strong believer in the peaceful protest of unjust laws. With the aid of Montgomery activists Jo Ann Robinson and the Women's Political Council, King put his ideas into practice with a boycott.

The MIA asked for three changes in the Montgomery public transportation system. The first was better treatment of African American passengers. The second was that seating should no longer be based on skin color. The third was to have black bus drivers

A FIRSTHAND LOOK AT

DR. KING AND HENRY DAVID THOREAU

The essay "**Civil Disobedience**," was written by poet and philosopher Henry David Thoreau in 1849. It inspired Martin Luther King Jr.'s beliefs in nonviolent protest. Thoreau wrote the essay during the heated debates about slavery that raged in the years before the Civil War. Thoreau argued that citizens should protest a government whose laws are unjust. Such protests should be "civil," or nonviolent. One of Thoreau's primary examples was slavery, which he strongly opposed. See page 60 for a link to view the complete contents of Thoreau's essay.

service routes that ran through African American neighborhoods. African Americans would not ride public buses until these three demands were met.

For 381 days, African Americans carpooled, rode bikes, or walked to and from work. The bus companies and downtown businesses suffered. The KKK, the police, and politicians tried to stop the boycott with threats, arrests, and violence. King's house was bombed. The boycott, however, continued.

Finally, on December 20, 1956, the Supreme Court ruled segregation on public buses was illegal. With this victory behind him, King and other southern ministers formed a new organization. In January 1957, they officially created the Southern Christian Leadership Conference (SCLC), with King as president. The SCLC would organize more peaceful protests, using them to inspire change across the country.

CHAPTER 2

STUDENTS TAKING ACTION

Businesses often displayed clear signs to let people know which race they served.

THE CONCEPT OF PEACEFUL
protest and civil disobedience caught on. People
in other cities organized bus boycotts. Peaceful
demonstrations took place across the South, as
both white and black Americans rallied behind
King.

Segregation rules were lifted for more schools
and bus systems. Restaurants, movie theaters,
and other public places, however, often remained
segregated. An African American could shop in
a department store but could not sit down to eat
at the lunch counter there. In the 1960s, college
students began to organize demonstrations to push
for equality in such places.

Protesters at sit-ins often had to endure abuse and insults from angry whites.

Segregated Lunches

In February 1960, four African American college students entered Woolworth's department store in Greensboro, North Carolina. Ignoring the "Reserved for Whites" sign, they each took a seat at the lunch counter. Though asked to leave, the four stayed until the store closed.

Word of this **sit-in** spread. Within days, sit-ins were taking place at other department stores and in other cities. Hundreds of people attended **rallies** and peaceful demonstrations in Greensboro. The African American population began a general boycott of segregated stores.

The protesters were met with anger. Food and coffee were poured over their heads. They were yanked off their stools and beaten. They were arrested, several of them more than once. But the protesters remained calm. They entered a store neatly dressed and sat down quietly. They stared straight ahead, never at their attackers. They did not move from their positions, even if a person beside them was dragged from a stool.

In Atlanta, Georgia, students Julian Bond and Lonnie King called for that city to organize its own sit-ins. In Nashville, Tennessee, student leader James Lawson explained proper sit-in behavior. This included remaining

YESTERDAY'S HEADLINES

Many people felt that segregation was normal. The separation of white and black people had been a part of life for generations in the South. One white southerner said, "Well, it's just not the things we're used to down here . . . we're not used to them [blacks] sitting down beside us, because I wasn't raised with them. I never have lived with them and I'm not going to start now." Some whites argued that restaurants were being denied their rights. They claimed that restaurants and lunch counters had the right to serve whomever they wished.

quiet, asking for help, supporting a team leader, and "remember[ing] love and nonviolence."

Giving In

As sit-ins spread, violence became worse. Protesters were arrested by the hundreds. Some were beaten or killed. In Atlanta, Georgia, someone threw acid in a protester's face. In Texas, a man was kidnapped, beaten, and left hanging upside down from a tree with "KKK" carved into his stomach. Policemen broke up rallies with the use of dogs, chains, and clubs.

Yet in the face of violence, the students bravely continued their protests. Within months, businesses were feeling the pressure. On July 25, the downtown

The KKK and other groups engaged in violence against the peaceful protesters.

The KKK often boycotted businesses that served African Americans.

stores in Greensboro admitted defeat. Stores in Nashville and other cities followed. Even the mayor of Nashville came to agree with the protesters. Lunch counters became integrated, and African Americans and whites were soon sitting and eating together.

In 1960, several students across the country organized the Student Nonviolent Coordinating Committee (SNCC). Anyone—white, African American, young, or old—could join. Thousands of people across the country did.

The Freedom Riders welcomed people of any racial background.

Freedom Riders

In 1961, an organization called the Congress of Racial Equality (CORE) decided to expand efforts against segregation. It would address the issue of buses traveling between states. Though legally integrated, buses and waiting rooms were still practicing segregation in the South. CORE planned a series of "Freedom Rides" to raise public awareness and inspire change.

CORE's director, James Farmer, informed the Federal Bureau of Investigation (FBI) of his plans. Because the buses and stations were legally integrated, the passengers, called Freedom Riders, would not be breaking any laws. White riders would sit in the back of the bus and African American riders in the front. African American riders would use the "white" restrooms, while white riders would use those labeled "colored."

On May 4, the first ride began in Washington, D.C., with two buses heading south toward New Orleans, Louisiana. The first 10 days of the ride were relatively peaceful. Then, after leaving Atlanta, Georgia, on May 14, one of the two buses was firebombed. Several Freedom Riders were hospitalized. The other bus was forced to stop in Birmingham, Alabama, by a gang of angry whites. The riders were beaten, and the bus drivers refused to take the riders any farther.

The Freedom Riders met with violent resistance from segregationists.

The National Guard was called in to protect Freedom Riders.

SNCC Takes Over

As the CORE rides ended, SNCC stepped in. U.S. attorney general Robert Kennedy supported the Freedom Riders. With his help, SNCC hired new bus drivers and received a promise of protection from the state of Alabama. But between Birmingham and Montgomery, the protection disappeared. Arriving in Montgomery, the riders were met by a mob. They were again beaten and several were hospitalized.

Kennedy called in federal marshals. Several civil rights leaders, including King, rallied in Montgomery to support the Freedom Riders. Violence against the riders and their supporters erupted in the city. Giving in to Kennedy's pressure, Alabama governor John Patterson finally sent in the Alabama National Guard to put down the violence.

The riders made it to Jackson, Mississippi. When they arrived at the station, they were taken to the local jail and then to the state prison for 60 days. Freedom Riders continued arriving in Jackson in more buses and continued to be arrested. By the end of the summer, Attorney General Kennedy called for the Interstate Commerce Commission to issue regulations to end segregation on buses that traveled across state lines. The regulations were set to take effect on November 1, 1961, but it would be two years before segregation in stations and buses ended across the South.

Walking through Birmingham

King traveled tirelessly throughout the South giving speeches and helping to organize demonstrations. He and the SCLC helped gain support and attention for civil rights efforts across the region.

In 1963, the SCLC turned its attention to Birmingham, Alabama, where lunch counters, movie theaters, and other businesses were still segregated. The city's government was in turmoil, with its elected leaders in the process of being driven out of office. King entered Birmingham in the midst of these troubles and organized a series of demonstrations. The SCLC organized a mass march, with hundreds of people walking through the streets carrying signs and singing songs. Boycotts and sit-ins were also organized. The demonstrations resulted in thousands of arrests that

Martin Luther King Jr. was jailed multiple times for peaceful protests.

overcrowded Birmingham jails. King was arrested more than once.

Many people felt the SCLC's protests were badly timed, because Birmingham was experiencing political upheaval. The demonstrations began to lose support. To reach Birmingham's adults, King and the SCLC turned to children. Older students were recruited, and they led marches. Thousands

A FIRSTHAND LOOK AT
THE "LETTER FROM BIRMINGHAM JAIL"

After being arrested and jailed in April 1963, Martin Luther King Jr. read a letter in a Birmingham newspaper written by eight white Alabama clergymen. They urged that the fight for civil rights take place in the courts and that the demonstrations stop. From his jail cell, King wrote a response, which has become known as the "Letter from Birmingham Jail." The letter explains why he continued his efforts, despite criticism. See page 60 for a link to view the full text of King's letter.

of young people participated. In an effort to stop the marches, Commissioner of Public Safety Eugene "Bull" Connor ordered his men to turn fire hoses on the demonstrators. The water from the high-pressure hoses knocked people off their feet and slammed them against walls or down upon the pavement. After one incident, some 2,500 protesters were arrested. Most of them were under the age of 18.

A VIEW FROM ABROAD

Eugene "Bull" Connor's actions did not go unnoticed. His use of fire hoses, police dogs, and clubs to fight the protesters was reported in newspapers internationally. Images of the violence against demonstrators, many of them children, shocked the world. People from many countries spoke out in support of the civil rights movement in the United States. They were impressed with Martin Luther King Jr.'s stance on conducting nonviolent demonstrations. In 1964, King was awarded the Nobel Peace Prize in Oslo, Norway.

Finally, with the eyes of the world watching, President John F. Kennedy, the brother of Attorney General Robert Kennedy, made an announcement. President Kennedy declared the situation in the South a "moral crisis." He announced that action had to be taken in Congress and that he would help push forward new civil rights laws.

CHAPTER 3

SECURING THE VOTE

King's "I Have a Dream" speech was one of the most influential events of the civil rights movement.

TO GAIN SUPPORT FOR KENNEDY'S
efforts to pass civil rights laws, the SCLC and
several other organizations put together a massive
march. On August 28, 1963, nearly 250,000 people
from all across America gathered at the Lincoln
Memorial in Washington, D.C. Here, at what is
known as the March on Washington, King gave his
famous "I Have a Dream" speech.

The civil rights movement was not fully unified.
SNCC's John Lewis was forced to edit comments
in his speech that were critical of the Kennedy
administration for being slow to take action on
civil rights. CORE's James Farmer was in jail in
Louisiana and could not participate in the march.

Four children were killed in the Birmingham church bombing.

Troubles

On Sunday, September 15, a bomb was thrown into the Sixteenth Avenue Baptist Church in Birmingham. The church had been a center for civil rights activities. Children were attending Sunday school classes when the bomb exploded. Four young African American girls were killed in the blast. The bombing was only one of many cases of the continued violence committed by the Ku Klux Klan and other white supremacists to halt the civil rights movement.

Two months after the church bombing, President Kennedy was **assassinated**. Vice President Lyndon Johnson became president. As a native southerner, many people feared—and some hoped—that he would work against civil rights. Over the next few years, however, Johnson showed he was a forceful and effective supporter of the civil rights movement.

Freedom Summer

Many state and local governments fought against the cause of civil rights. In the South, states passed laws that made it almost impossible for African Americans to vote. The 15th Amendment guaranteed them the right to vote, but southern states required people to pass a test in order to **register**. Whites who often could

"Freedom Schools" helped African Americans find ways to get around the unfair practices that kept them from voting.

not even read judged these tests. Many areas required voters to pay a tax to register. If tests and taxes didn't work to prevent African Americans from voting, then government officials and white citizens resorted to threats or violence.

As a result, only 43 percent of African Americans in the United States old enough to vote were registered. In Mississippi, only 6.7 percent were registered. Without the vote, African Americans had no political power to change laws. CORE, SNCC, and the SCLC decided to do something to correct the situation. In June 1964, Freedom Summer was announced. It was a plan to "open up Mississippi" by helping African Americans register to vote.

Black voters turned out in huge numbers for the 1964 elections.

Going to Mississippi

Volunteers for the project were both white and black. Most attended universities in the North. They attended training sessions in Ohio to learn how to respond to mobs and were warned about the probability of violence. Three of the first volunteers sent to Mississippi were arrested one day. When they were released late that night, they disappeared. All three were later found dead.

This tragedy did not stop the volunteers. Hundreds traveled to Mississippi and held voter registration drives, passed out flyers, and went door-to-door to get African Americans to register. The Freedom Summer volunteers helped create the new Mississippi Freedom Democratic Party, and

YESTERDAY'S HEADLINES

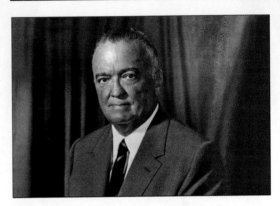

After the three Freedom Summer volunteers disappeared in June 1964, there was debate about offering other volunteers protection. J. Edgar Hoover (above), the head of the Federal Bureau of Investigation (FBI), refused. The FBI investigates crimes, he argued. He thought protection should be taken care of by local law enforcement.

The governor of Mississippi would not offer protection, either. He considered the waves of volunteers an invasion of the state. Instead of calling in police and highway patrol to protect the volunteers, they were called in to protect Mississippi from the volunteers.

President Johnson signs the Civil Rights Act. It was a major step forward for the movement.

about 80,000 Mississippians joined. Many volunteers were beaten, but they continued with their work peacefully.

Meanwhile, the law that President Kennedy had promised to pass the previous year was finally a reality. In July, President Johnson signed into law the Civil Rights Act of 1964. This act required businesses to give equal opportunity to people applying for jobs. It also officially outlawed all forms of segregation in public places.

Voting in Alabama

SNCC and the SCLC also worked to help voters register in Alabama. They focused their efforts on Selma. In 1965, more than one-half of Selma's population was African American, but only 1 percent of them were registered to vote. Beginning on January 22, marches were organized by several groups. People from all walks of life took part.

The marchers were faced with violent resistance from ordinary citizens and from Sheriff Jim Clark.

During a nighttime march, a mob attacked the protesters. Jimmy Lee Jackson, one of the protesters, was shot dead by a state trooper while trying to protect his mother. Angry and frustrated, the SCLC organized

The march from Selma to Montgomery was met with violence.

YESTERDAY'S HEADLINES

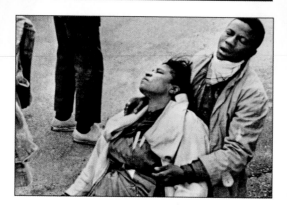

The night after civil rights marchers were attacked on Selma's Edmund Pettus Bridge, video of the violence was shown on televisions across America. Viewers saw frightening images of protesters being beaten and showered in tear gas. Government leaders, including the U.S. attorney general and the governor of Texas, expressed shock and outrage. Alabama law enforcement had gone too far.

a massive march from Selma to Montgomery. It would be a five- or six-day walk.

Alabama's governor, George Wallace, banned the march. SNCC opposed the march and did not participate, though SNCC leader John Lewis did. The marchers gathered on Sunday, March 7, and began their walk through Selma. When they reached Edmund Pettus Bridge, the marchers were stopped by the police. When the marchers did not leave, they were attacked with clubs, cattle prods, whips, and tear gas.

Marching Forward

The SCLC wanted to go on with the march, starting again in Selma. President Johnson, however, asked them to wait. Federal judge Frank Johnson ordered them not to march until there was an investigation into the violence. With support from SNCC, King announced that they had "gone too far now to turn back." The event went forward on March 9. More people joined in, including politicians and SNCC. When stopped again at Pettus Bridge, the Reverend Ralph Abernathy led a prayer, and the marchers turned back. That evening, one of the marchers, the Reverend James Reeb, was severely beaten and died days later.

When demonstrators tried again to march, they were blocked by law enforcement. Johnson asked Congress for support, using the slogan of the movement, "We shall overcome." Then, on March 17, the participants were given a legal **permit** to march. Violence against the demonstrators continued, but the march moved forward.

To protect the marchers, President Johnson sent in 2,200 members of the National Guard. More than 25,000 marchers participated. Politicians, religious leaders, celebrities, and children marched. As they marched, SNCC members took the opportunity to work with members of the surrounding communities.

A FIRSTHAND LOOK AT
THE MARCH ON WASHINGTON

The historic March on Washington was a defining moment in the civil rights movement. The events of that day were captured on film, in recordings, and in countless newspaper and magazine articles around the world. See page 60 for a link to view photos and video of the event, to read the speeches of Martin Luther King Jr. and John Lewis, and to read newspaper editorials commenting on the historic gathering.

CHAPTER 4

PRIDE AND POWER

President Lyndon Johnson (right) chats with Senator Everett Dirksen (center) and Vice President Hubert Humphrey (left) after signing the Voting Rights Act in 1965.

On August 6, 1965,

President Johnson signed the new Voting Rights Act into law. The act outlawed all discriminatory voting practices, which had prevented many African Americans from voting. Thousands of African Americans registered to vote. By 1969, 61 percent of African Americans who were able to vote were registered.

But the news was not all good. As marchers were making their way from Montgomery back to Selma, one of their drivers was murdered by the KKK. Differences between SNCC and the SCLC were pulling the two organizations apart. In cities in the North, many people began to believe that nonviolence was not working quickly or effectively enough.

The Nation of Islam took a different approach to civil rights than peaceful protesters such as Martin Luther King Jr. had.

Urban Problems

In northern cities, poverty and a poor education system gave African Americans few opportunities to escape from urban slums. Drugs and crime were widespread in some of these poor neighborhoods.

In the midst of this grew the Nation of Islam (NOI), a religious organization founded by Wali Fard Muhammad. Muhammad preached pride, unity, and self-sufficiency within the African American community. Its members, known as Black Muslims, followed strict rules about behavior, dress, and treatment of women.

The NOI urged separation of the African American community from the white community. Nonviolence was not something they necessarily believed in. Malcolm X, a minister in the NOI, preached that rights and personal protection should be secured "by any means necessary."

Voting in Alabama

The Lowndes County Freedom Organization was formed in Alabama to counteract the white supremacist Democratic Party in the state. Its symbol was a black panther. The political party was organized by SNCC leader Stokely Carmichael. When the party's candidates ran for office in Lowndes County in 1965, about 3,900 people voted for them.

The Black Panthers, as they became known, were viewed as a **militant** group within SNCC. In May 1966,

SPOTLIGHT ON

Malcolm X

Born Malcolm Little in Omaha, Nebraska, in 1925, Malcolm X was the son of a civil rights leader. His father died when Malcolm was six. Malcolm dropped out of school and turned to crime. He was arrested and jailed in 1946.

In prison, he was introduced to the teachings of Elijah Muhammad, the leader of the Nation of Islam. After he was released from prison, he became an NOI minister. In 1964, he left the NOI to create Muslim Mosque, Inc., and later changed his name to El Hajj Malik El Shabazz.

The Black Panthers often dressed in military uniforms.

Carmichael was voted national chairman of SNCC, taking over from John Lewis. Carmichael believed in a more assertive approach to civil rights, saying "I'm not going to beg the white man for anything I deserve. I'm going to take it." Carmichael's phrase "black power" became a new motto for the movement.

Dissent and Separation

SNCC's new approach soon became apparent in Mississippi. Demonstrator James Meredith had organized a march in the state to support voter registration. When he was shot, SNCC and the SCLC decided to continue the march. Meredith survived the shooting.

The Meredith marchers were beaten, showered in tear gas, and arrested. After he was released from jail, Carmichael expressed his frustration. "Black Power" was chanted by his followers and was later adopted by CORE.

Rise of Riots

In 1965, violence erupted in the mainly black neighborhood of Watts in Los Angeles, California. The trouble began when a man named Marquette Frye was being arrested for driving drunk. A fight broke out, which turned into a raging mob. The mob looted and burned the neighborhood for days. Thirty-four

Entire buildings were destroyed during the Los Angeles riots.

people were killed, and $40 million in property damage was caused. It took 22,500 police supported by 14,000 members of the National Guard to put a halt to the rioting.

Americans were afraid the riots would spread to other cities. In an effort to curb the violence, King went on a tour of urban slums. In Chicago, a young activist named Jesse Jackson was sent to run SCLC's new Operation Breadbasket, an organization begun to improve the economic conditions of African American communities. Jackson and King tried to encourage peaceful protests, but the communities showed little interest. Many were listening instead to the arguments of the NOI, Stokely Carmichael, and the rising voice of the Black Panther Party.

National Guardsmen rounded up rioters in Watts.

Black Panthers

Police violence against African Americans in cities grew with the threat of more riots. In response, Huey Newton and Bobby Seale organized the Black Panther Party for Self Defense (later named the Black Panther Party) in California in 1966. Their beliefs were inspired by revolutions going on in Latin America and the growing militancy in the American civil rights movement. They carried guns and were not afraid to defend themselves and others in the community.

YESTERDAY'S HEADLINES

In 1954, the United States became involved in a war that was taking place in the Southeast Asian country of Vietnam. Thousands of American troops were sent to fight. As U.S. involvement increased, bitter divisions developed back home. Many Americans argued against the war, while others claimed the war should be fought to stop the spread of **communism**. Many people thought that the war drew attention away from the issues of poverty and the fight for civil rights in the United States.

The Black Panthers worked within poor African American communities to educate residents about their legal rights. At the same time, they monitored the actions of the local police to prevent further violence. Many people, including teenagers, were dissatisfied with the lack of change in the cities and joined the Panthers.

Steps Continue

In 1967, riots broke out in other cities across the United States, including Detroit, Michigan; Chicago, Illinois; Cincinnati, Ohio; and New York. Yet even as the violence spread, peaceful victories were still taking place in the late 1960s. In Cleveland, Ohio, Carl Stokes was voted the city's first African American mayor. Richard Hatcher of Gary, Indiana, and Charles Evers of Fayette, Mississippi, were also elected mayor. The NAACP's Thurgood Marshall was appointed to the U.S. Supreme Court, becoming the first African American to hold a seat on the nation's highest court.

"I Am a Man"

Sanitation workers in Memphis, Tennessee, wanted better treatment and higher wages. The workers went on strike with picket signs announcing, "I Am a Man."

A FIRSTHAND LOOK AT
THE KING ASSASSINATION

The worldwide reaction to the assassination of Dr. Martin Luther King Jr. was shock. Many people around the world found it hard to believe that King should meet such a violent end after preaching and practicing nonviolence for years. See page 60 for a link to an article about King's death and to hear a report from Great Britain made on the day of his assassination.

Martin Luther King Jr. (second from right) died at the Lorraine Motel in Tennessee.

When workers did not get what they demanded, King and the SCLC were called in to help. A march was organized, but it turned into a riot. Feeling defeated, King left Memphis, but he returned several weeks later.

On April 3, 1968, he gave a speech at a large rally in Memphis to gain support for a new march. The next day, he was shot dead on the balcony of his room at the Lorraine Motel. The shock echoed around the world.

Two months later, on June 5, former attorney general Robert Kennedy was also assassinated. At the time he was campaigning to become president. The two deaths marked a tragic end to the era when the fight for civil rights for African Americans filled the streets, the newspapers, and the hearts of Americans.

What Happened Where?

WA

ND

MT

OR

ID

SD

WY

NV

UT

CO

KS

CA

NE

Watts, Los Angeles, California A riot in Watts in 1965 sets off a string of riots across the United States.

● **Los Angeles**
(Watts neighborhood)

AZ

NM

OK

TX

N
W ● E
S

AK

HI

Little Rock, Arkansas In 1957, the Little Rock Nine, with the help of NAACP member Daisy Lee Gatson Bates, become the first African American students to attend a white school in the South.

Memphis, Tennessee Martin Luther King Jr. is shot at the Lorraine Motel in 1968 by James Earl Ray.

Washington, D.C. Martin Luther King Jr. delivers his "I Have a Dream" speech during the March on Washington in 1963.

Greensboro, North Carolina In 1960, Joseph McNeill, Franklin McCain, Ezell Blair, and David Richmond sit down at a lunch counter, setting off a string of sit-ins across the South.

Birmingham, Alabama Freedom Riders are attacked in 1961, and the police use fire hoses against demonstrators in 1963.

Selma, Alabama Freedom Riders are attacked in 1961.

Jackson, Mississippi The Freedom Riders are stopped in Jackson and arrested in 1961.

New Orleans, Louisiana The intended final destination of the Freedom Rides.

ME
VT
NH
NY
MA
CT
RI
WI
MI
PA
IA
NJ
OH
Washington, D.C.
IL
IN
DE
WV
MD
MO
VA
KY
Greensboro
TN
NC
AR
Memphis
SC
Little Rock
AL
GA
MS
Birmingham
Selma
Montgomery
Jackson
LA
New Orleans
FL

0   150   300 mi
0   150   300 km

The Ongoing Quest for Equality

The fight for civil rights continues to this day. Schools, businesses, and neighborhoods still struggle with the tasks of integration and achieving equality.

Although many people believe that progress has not been swift enough, progress has indeed been made. At one time in the United States, African Americans had no rights. They were the property of others. But with each passing generation, hard-won rights were obtained and exercised. The walls of segregation were slowly broken down.

In the past, African Americans did not have the right to vote, and when they gained that right, they experienced discrimination at the polls. But since the 1960s, seven African Americans have run for president of the United States. None won until 2008, when Illinois senator Barack Obama received almost 70 million votes and became the first African American president of the United States.

African American civil rights are not the only rights that have been called into question in the history of the United States. Efforts to gain rights for women took place throughout the 20th century and continue even today. The rights of immigrants and gay people are headline news on a nearly daily basis. Over the last several decades, important strides have been made in the treatment and rights of people with disabilities. Employment, housing, education, marriage, and military laws continue to change in order to better provide equality for all citizens.

Barack Obama was elected president in 2008.

Lyndon B. Johnson (1908–1973) was president from 1963 to 1969. He signed the Voting Rights Act into law in 1965.

Thurgood Marshall (1908–1993) was a leader in the NAACP and a successful civil rights lawyer. He was nominated by two presidents before officially becoming a Supreme Court judge in 1967.

Rosa Parks

Rosa Parks (1913–2005) was a civil rights activist in Montgomery, Alabama. She inspired and took part in the city's bus boycotts in 1955 and 1956. Parks has been called the "mother of the civil rights movement."

John F. Kennedy (1917–1963) was president from 1961 until his assassination in 1963. He was a supporter of civil rights.

John F. Kennedy

Malcolm X (1925–1965) was a minister with the Nation of Islam until he left the group in 1964. After a trip to the Middle East, his beliefs changed to become more inclusive, and he started Muslim Mosque, Inc.

Robert F. Kennedy (1925–1968) was U.S. attorney general and a supporter of civil rights. While campaigning for president in 1968, he was assassinated.

Martin Luther King Jr. (1929–1968) was perhaps the most famous leader of the civil rights movement. He preached a policy of nonviolence. King helped form the SCLC in 1957 and fought for civil rights until his assassination in 1968.

John Lewis (1940–) helped organize SNCC and later became its chairman. He was a major leader throughout the civil rights movement and beyond.

Stokely Carmichael (1941–1998) was a member of SNCC and became its chairman in 1966. He helped form the Lowndes County Freedom Organization.

Stokely Carmichael

TIMELINE

1865
The 13th Amendment is passed, ending slavery.

1868
The 14th Amendment is passed, making African Americans equal citizens.

1870
The 15th Amendment is passed, giving African American men the right to vote.

1896
Plessy v. Ferguson establishes the practice of "separate but equal."

1960
February
Students begin holding sit-ins in Greensboro, North Carolina.

April
The Student Nonviolent Coordinating Committee forms.

1961
The Freedom Rides begin.

1963
April
Martin Luther King Jr. leads marches on Birmingham, Alabama.

August 28
The March on Washington takes place.

September 15
The Sixteenth Avenue Baptist Church in Birmingham is bombed.

1964
Freedom Summer begins in June; President Johnson signs the Civil Rights Act of 1964 into law in July.

1954

Brown v. Board of Education of Topeka, Kansas, legally ends segregation in schools.

1955

The Montgomery bus boycott begins.

1956

The U.S. Supreme Court rules segregation on city buses is illegal.

1957

The Southern Christian Leadership Conference is formed.

September
The Little Rock Nine begin attending Little Rock Central High School.

1965

March
The SCLC and SNCC leaders lead a march from Selma to Montgomery.

August 6
The Voting Rights Act is signed into law.

A riot breaks out in Watts, in Los Angeles, California.

1966

June
The SCLC and SNCC lead the Meredith march.

1967

Race riots spread throughout the country; the cities of Cleveland and Gary vote in their first African American mayors; Thurgood Marshall becomes the first African American U.S. Supreme Court justice.

1968

April 4
Martin Luther King Jr. is assassinated.

June 6
Robert Kennedy dies after being shot the day before.

LIVING HISTORY

Primary sources provide firsthand evidence about a topic. Witnesses to a historical event create primary sources. They include autobiographies, newspaper reports of the time, oral histories, photographs, and memoirs. A secondary source analyzes primary sources, and is one step or more removed from the event. Secondary sources include textbooks, encyclopedias, and commentaries.

The Assassination of Dr. Martin Luther King Jr. To read an article about the assassination of King on April 4, 1968, and to hear an audio report about the events in Memphis and throughout the United States that day, go to *http://news.bbc.co.uk/onthisday/hi/dates/stories /april/4/newsid_2453000/2453987.stm*

Henry David Thoreau's "Civil Disobedience" To read the complete text of Thoreau's influential "Civil Disobedience" essay, go to *http://thoreau.eserver.org/civil.html*

The March on Washington To view photos and videos, and to read speeches from the historic March on Washington, on August 28, 1963, go to *www.pbs.org/wgbh/amex/eyesontheprize/story/08_ washington.html#music*

Martin Luther King Jr.'s "Letter from Birmingham Jail" To view King's response to a call to halt demonstrations in Birmingham, go to *http://mlk-kpp01.stanford.edu/index.php/resources/article /annotated_letter_from_birmingham/*

Books

Gold, Susan Dudley. *The Civil Rights Act of 1964*. New York: Marshall Cavendish Benchmark, 2011.

Gosman, Gillian. *Martin Luther King Jr.* New York: PowerKids Press, 2011.

Hardy, Sheila, and P. Stephen Hardy. *Extraordinary People of the Civil Rights Movement*. New York: Children's Press, 2007.

Magoon, Kekla. *Today the World Is Watching You: The Little Rock Nine and the Fight for School Integration, 1957*. Minneapolis: Twenty-first Century Books, 2011.

Stokes, John A., Lois Wolfe, and Herman J. Viola. *Students on Strike: Jim Crow, Civil Rights, Brown, and Me: A Memoir*. Washington, DC: National Geographic, 2008.

Tougas, Shelley. *Birmingham 1963: How a Photograph Rallied Civil Rights Support*. Mankota, MN: Compass Point Books, 2011.

Web Sites

National Association for the Advancement of Colored People
www.naacp.org/
This site includes information on the NAACP's history as well as descriptions of current projects and activities.

National Park Service—We Shall Overcome
www.nps.gov/nr/travel/civilrights/
Check out important historical places in the civil rights movement. Learn about the movement's people, strategies, and major events.

PBS American Experience—Eyes on the Prize
www.pbs.org/wgbh/amex/eyesontheprize/
Check out this site for videos, primary sources, important dates and events, and much more about the civil rights movement.

GLOSSARY

activist (AK-tihv-ist) a person who works to support or oppose a cause or an issue

assassinated (uh-SASS-uh-nay-ted) murdered, usually someone well known

boycott (BOI-kaht) refusing to buy goods from a person, group, or country

civil disobedience (SIV-uhl diss-oh-BEE-dee-unss) disobeying a law peacefully, particularly if the law is believed to be unjust

civil rights (SIV-uhl RITES) the rights belonging to a nation's citizens

communism (KAHM-yuh-niz-uhm) a way of organizing a country's economy so that all the property, business, and resources belong to the government or community, and the profits are shared by all

diversity (di-VUR-suh-tee) having difference or variety

integrate (IN-tuh-grate) to include people of all races

militant (MIL-uh-tuhnt) encouraging or representing an aggressive stance

permit (PUR-mit) a legal document granting permission

rallies (RAL-eez) large gatherings, usually for political reasons

register (REJ-uh-stur) to enter one's name on an official list

segregate (SEG-ruh-gate) to separate or keep people apart

sit-in (SIT-in) a form of peaceful protest in which one sits at a place usually forbidden

supremacists (suh-PREM-uh-sists) people who believe that a group is superior to another group

INDEX

Page numbers in *italics* indicate illustrations.

ABOUT THE AUTHOR

Jennifer Zeiger graduated from DePaul University, where she studied English and religion. She now writes and edits children's books in Chicago.